ROALD DAHL

The BFG

PLAYS *for* CHILDREN

ADAPTED BY DAVID WOOD

PUFFIN

Find out more about Roald Dahl and the adapted plays by visiting the websites roalddahl.com and davidwood.org.uk

PERFORMANCE RIGHTS:
All rights whatsoever in these plays are strictly reserved, and application for performance, etc., should be made before rehearsals commence to: (for amateur stage performance) Samuel French Limited, 52 Fitzroy Street, London WIT 5JR; (for all other performance rights) Casarotto Ramsay & Associates Ltd, Waverley House, 7–12 Noel Street, London WIF 8GQ.

No performances may be given unless a licence has been obtained. The publication of these plays does not necessarily indicate their availability for performance.

PUFFIN BOOKS

Published by the Penguin Group
Penguin Books Ltd, 80 Strand, London WC2R ORL, England
Penguin Group (USA) Inc., 375 Hudson Street, New York, New York 10014, USA
Penguin Group (Canada), 90 Eglinton Avenue East, Suite 700, Toronto, Ontario, Canada M4P 2Y3
(a division of Pearson Penguin Canada Inc.)
Penguin Ireland, 25 St Stephen's Green, Dublin 2, Ireland (a division of Penguin Books Ltd)
Penguin Group (Australia), 707 Collins Street, Melbourne, Victoria 3008, Australia
(a division of Pearson Australia Group Pty Ltd)
Penguin Books India Pvt Ltd, 11 Community Centre, Panchsheel Park, New Delhi – 110 017, India
Penguin Group (NZ), 67 Apollo Drive, Rosedale, Auckland 0632, New Zealand
(a division of Pearson New Zealand Ltd)
Penguin Books (South Africa) (Pty) Ltd, Block D, Rosebank Office Park, 181 Jan Smuts Avenue, Parktown North,
Gauteng 2193, South Africa

Penguin Books Ltd, Registered Offices: 80 Strand, London WC2R ORL, England

puffinbooks.com

First published 1993
Reissued 2001, 2009 and 2014
001

Text copyright © Roald Dahl Nominee Ltd and David Wood, 1993
Title-page illustrations © Quentin Blake, 2009
Main text illustrations copyright © Jane Walmsley, 1993
Title-page illustrations copyright © Quentin Blake, 2014
All rights reserved

The moral right of the author and illustrators has been asserted

Set in Monotype Baskerville
Typeset by Datix International Ltd, Bungay, Suffolk
Printed in Great Britain by Clays Ltd, St Ives plc

British Library Cataloguing in Publication Data
A CIP catalogue record for this book is available from the British Library

ISBN: 978-0-140-36367-8

www.greenpenguin.co.uk

CONTENTS

For
Sophie Barnes and Daniel Leuw
with love from
the Godfather

David Wood would like to thank Justin Savage and James Woods
of Clarion Productions for originally commissioning him
to adapt the full-length play *The BFG*, and for producing it
in London's West End and on tour.

Susie Caulcutt designed the first professional production of The BFG. David Wood wishes to acknowledge that her visual conception of his play helped him plan *The BFG: Plays for Children*.

FOREWORD

When he had finished correcting the last proof of *The BFG*, my husband turned to me and said, 'Liccy, if there is a classic amongst my books, I think this is it.' He looked happy and relaxed. He stood up from his great chair, fetched a golf-club and went into the orchard to hit some golf balls. One of these golf balls landed in front of our bedroom window, a distance of 194 metres – a fair drive. In his youth he was a scratch golfer.

Why was *The BFG* such a favourite? For many reasons. He suffered from insomnia and would lie for hours creating his own dreams of glory. For example, playing cricket for England. As the number eleven batsman he would walk down the steps of the pavilion, across the outfield and up to the crease. The crowds would gasp at the sight of this handsome, untidy sixty-five-year-old man with a limp. Who was he? Had the captain gone mad? How could this old man save England? Well, of course, he did. He struck each ball with a straight bat and hey presto, every time a boundary. There was no stopping him. In no time at all the match was won. The Queen gave him a huge medal and he rode in an open-topped bus all over England, the crowds waving and cheering. He was their hero. Another reason: he longed for Mr Schweppes to manufacture the frobscottle so that everyone would be whizzpopping down the high street, and in their classrooms, etc.

But personally, I think he was trying to tell us how beastly the human 'bean' can be − a warning to you all. The world needs heroes like the BFG. Perhaps one day you will be a hero and a big friendly human bean. I do hope so. In the mean time, keep reading the book and enjoy performing the plays.

Felicity Dahl

INTRODUCTION

Roald Dahl had a mission to encourage children to read books. The huge popularity of his stories is a measure of his success.

My aim as a playwright is to introduce children to the excitement of live theatre. So the invitation to adapt *The BFG* for the stage was a challenge I couldn't resist. The very title would be enough to entice many teachers and parents to bring children to see the play. But for me it brought a tremendous responsibility to translate the book faithfully from page to stage, to avoid devoted fans of the book being disappointed.

Happily the play has been successful on tour and in London's West End, and, as a result, several teachers and parents suggested I might further adapt *The BFG* as a group of short plays for children to read and maybe perform themselves.

Thanks to Puffin Books, here they are! I have tried to make them varied in length. Some give the opportunity for a whole class or group of children to take part; some have a smaller cast for more experienced players. All can be staged without complicated scenery or effects. Some are suitable for one-act-play festivals. Above all I have tried to make them fun – it has always seemed to me no coincidence that the word 'play' has two meanings.

The problem of scale has to be faced when adapting and performing a story about a small girl and a seven-metre-high giant! The solution is really quite straightforward. In the Giant Country plays, all the giants, including the BFG, are played by human beings, but Sophie is played by a doll or puppet, operated and spoken by an actress. In the Buckingham Palace ballroom play, human beings are played by human beings and the BFG has to be really big! A giant puppet is possible, but tricky; an actor up a step-ladder looking over a painted flat could work; or we could even *imagine* the giant BFG off stage. I'm sure many similarly inventive ways of doing it can be thought of.

Finally, I'd like to say how whoopsey-splunkers it was to write these plays, based on such a scrumdiddlyumptious book. May you have a glumptious time reading and performing them.

David Wood

THE SNATCHING OF SOPHIE

This short play can involve a whole class or group, yet the main focus is on the performance of just two actors. It could be ideal for introducing young people to the idea of acting out a story. If they enjoy this comparatively straightforward scene, they may be encouraged to go on to something more complex.

CHARACTERS

Six actors: can be dressed in their own clothes, or in a 'uniform' like jeans and T-shirts. (Actor 5, who almost 'becomes' Sophie, could be dressed in night-dress and glasses, like the *Sophie doll* she carries. But it is not essential.)

The BFG: should wear a shirt, waistcoat, trousers, belt and sandals, as described in the book. He should also wear a lightweight cloak.

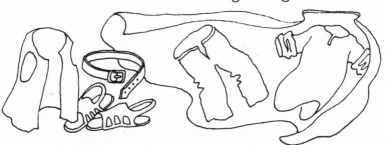

SETTING
An empty space.

SPECIAL PROPS
The Sophie doll: doll in a nightdress and glasses
to represent Sophie.

A doll's house: this should be able to open to
receive the Sophie doll, and have a window
through which the BFG can snatch it.

The BFG's suitcase: containing a dream jar.

The BFG's trumpet or dream-blowing horn: should be attachable to his suitcase.

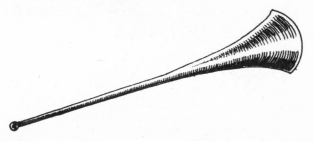

A dream jar: an interestingly shaped jar or bottle, preferably not breakable! It should be painted a bright colour.

A torch.

SOUND EFFECTS

None is essential, but it might be worth trying the sound of a mysterious howling wind underneath the 'Running, striding, leaping' unison speech.

The fanfares could be played on an instrument or vocalized by actors. And sinister music could accompany the BFG's entrance. Woodblocks or xylophone could suggest the passage of time.

LIGHTING

No special lighting is required, but it would be effective to lower the levels for the entrance of the BFG, or pick him out in his own light.

THE SNATCHING OF SOPHIE

Curtain up.

The CAST, *all except the* BFG, *assembles in a semi-circle. Most of the actors will remain in position watching the action, which takes place in front of them. The doll's house is to one side. Fanfare.*

ALL: The BFG, by Roald Dahl.
[*Fanfare*]

The beginning of the story.
[*Fanfare*]

The snatching of Sophie.

ACTOR 1: It was late at night . . .

ACTOR 2: [*Makes an owl hooting noise*]

ACTOR 3: . . . in the orphanage.
[ACTOR 4 *brings the doll's house to the centre, and stays with it*]

ACTOR 5: [*Coming forward holding up the* SOPHIE DOLL] In the dormitory, Sophie couldn't sleep.
[ACTOR 4 *opens the doll's house*]

[ACTOR 5 *puts the* SOPHIE DOLL *inside*]

[ACTOR 4 *closes the doll's house, then returns to the semicircle*]

[ACTOR 5 *now becomes the main* NARRATOR, *acting out the story as she tells it*]

ACTOR 5: A brilliant moonbeam was shining right on to her pillow.
[ACTOR 6 *switches on a torch and shines it through the doll's house upstairs window*]

She slipped out of bed to get a drink of water.

ACTOR 6: Sophie! Back to bed this instant. You know the rules.

ACTOR 5: Mrs Clonkers! Sophie went back to bed. She tried very hard to doze off. The time ticked by.
[ACTOR 7 *plays a tick-tock noise on wood-blocks or a xylophone*]

The house was absolutely silent. Perhaps, thought Sophie, this is what they call the witching hour, that special moment in the middle of the night when everyone is in a deep, deep sleep, and all the dark things come out from hiding and have the world to themselves. She crept to the window. And suddenly she saw . . . a giant!
[ACTOR 8, *in a cloak and carrying a suitcase,*

appears as the BFG. *He comes through the semicircle. The* ACTORS *crouch down in awe. The* BFG *looms over the doll's house, then proceeds downstage, acting out the narration*]

He stopped at the house opposite, bent down to look in a bedroom window and then . . .

[*The* BFG *opens his suitcase, takes out a jar and pours its contents into the end of a horn-like trumpet. Then he blows through it into the imaginary window. All the* ACTORS *make the blowing noise. The* BFG *replaces the jar in his case and reattaches the trumpet. He turns towards the doll's house*]

[*With a gasp*] He saw Sophie. She pulled back from the window, flew across the dormitory and jumped into her bed and hid under the blanket, tingling all over.

[*The* BFG *approaches the doll's house. He peeps in the window and, with a growl, pushes his hand through and snatches the* SOPHIE DOLL, *holding it up high*]

Aaaaaaaah!

[*The* BFG *tucks the* SOPHIE DOLL *inside his cloak and stands centre. He begins slow-motion, on-the-spot running, echoing the following description*]

ACTORS: [*In unison*] Running, striding, leaping through the night. Over fields, over hedges, over rivers, each stride as long as a tennis-court. Faster, faster, feet scarcely touching the ground. Over oceans, over forests, over mountains . . .

[*The* BFG *slows down and exits through the semicircle*]

[*Slowly standing up again*] To a land unknown to human beings.

[*Curtain down*]

SOPHIE IN GIANT COUNTRY

In this play, the BFG and Sophie get to know each other. At first the atmosphere between them is tense, then it relaxes somewhat. This contrasts with the growing tension amongst the other giants, leading to a savage child-eating raid.

CHARACTERS

Sophie: the actress should be dressed like the Sophie doll she carries, in night-dress and glasses. She talks 'through' the doll. It is important that the BFG always looks at the doll and *never* at the actress!

The BFG: wearing shirt, waistcoat, belt, trousers and sandals. His cloak is optional.

The Giants: Fleshlumpeater, Bloodbottler, Bonecruncher, Childchewer, Meatdripper and Gizzardgulper (all with speaking roles).

Other Giants: (without individual lines) if required, including Butcher Boy, Maidmasher, Manhugger. All the giants could wear sacking tunics, or 'basic' jeans and dark T-shirts. The most important part of their costume is the masks, each of which should be different and as horrible as possible. Head-dresses could be used, attached to a 'helmet', as illustrated. By lowering the head, the actor's own head becomes invisible; also, the voice can be heard more clearly.

SETTING

To one side of the performing area is *the BFG's cave*. This can be simply achieved with a table and stool. A more sophisticated cave is possible, though not necessary, with shelves of dream jars, rock-like walls and an entrance.

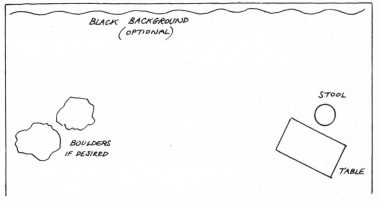

The other side − the main acting area − represents *Giant Country*. It needs no scenery at all, but a number of boulders for the giants to sit on could be useful. Black flats or curtains might make a good background.

SPECIAL PROPS

The Sophie doll: dressed in a night-dress and glasses. She could be a puppet on a central rod, with another rod to operate her arm.

'Human Bean' dolls: a selection of soft-toy dolls for the giants to 'eat'. They should be lying upstage ready to be discovered.

SOUND EFFECTS

None is necessary, but percussion or exciting music could be used for the sinister giant episodes.

LIGHTING

No special lighting is required, but it would be effective to distinguish between the cave area and the giants' area. The cave should seem cosy in contrast to the sinister atmosphere of Giant Country, which could perhaps be red or green. When the giants advance to find 'human beans', a flashing light or 'strobe' effect would be exciting.

SOPHIE IN GIANT COUNTRY

Curtain up.

Before the play proper begins, SOPHIE *shows the audience the* SOPHIE DOLL.

SOPHIE: This is Sophie, an orphan. One night, from her dormitory window, she sees ... a giant!

[*Enter the* BFG. *He snatches the* SOPHIE DOLL *and carries it to the cave*]

He snatches her and, terrified, she finds herself carried off to a strange country unknown to human beings.

[SOPHIE *goes to the cave and kneels at the table as the* BFG *puts the* SOPHIE DOLL *down.* SOPHIE *takes the* SOPHIE DOLL *and manipulates it like a puppet, while providing* SOPHIE'S *voice*]

BFG: [*Standing over the* SOPHIE DOLL] Ha! What has us got here?

[*He looks carefully at the* SOPHIE DOLL. *At first he should not appear very friendly*]

SOPHIE: [*Nervously*] Where am I?

BFG: This is my cave.

SOPHIE: Why did you snatch me and bring me here?

BFG: Because you *saw* me. If anyone is ever *seeing* a giant, he or she must be taken away hipswitch.

SOPHIE: Why?

BFG: Human beans is not *believing* in giants, is they? Human beans is not *thinking* giants exist.

SOPHIE: I do.

BFG: Ah, but that is because you has *seen* me. If I hadn't snitched you, you would be scuddling around yodelling the news on the telly-telly bunkum box that you were actually *seeing* a giant, and then a great giant-hunt, a mighty giant look-see, would be starting up all over the world, and human beans would be trying to catch me and put me in the zoo with all those squiggling hippodumplings and croca-downdillies.

SOPHIE: So what's going to happen to me now?

BFG: You will just have to be staying here with me for the rest of your life.

SOPHIE: Oh no!

BFG: Oh yes! Now, I is hungry!

SOPHIE: [*Gasping*] Please don't eat me!

BFG: [*Bellowing with laughter*] Just because I is a giant, you think I is a man-gobbling canny-bull! No!

SOPHIE: Oh, good.

BFG: Yes, you is lucky. If one of the other giants is snitching you, they is crunching you up for sure. In one scrumdiddlyumptious mouthful. Bones crackety-crackety-cracking. Gobble, gobbledy, gone!

SOPHIE: Other giants? You mean there are more of you?

BFG: Of course! This is Giant Country! [*He picks up the* SOPHIE DOLL] Be peeping out over there, little girl, and be seeing a brain-bogglingsome sight.
> [*He carries the doll to the cave entrance.* SOPHIE *follows. They peep out at the other side, where the other* GIANTS *appear, lumbering about, looking menacing and hungry, grunting and occasionally threatening one another. They make themselves identifiable as the* BFG *mentions them*]

SOPHIE: Gosh!

BFG: Is you believing your gogglers?

SOPHIE: What on earth are they doing?

BFG: Nothing. They is just moocheling and footcheling around and waiting for the night to come. Then they will be galloping off to places where human beans is living to find chiddlers to guzzle for their suppers.

SOPHIE: Where?

BFG: All over the world.

BONECRUNCHER: I is fancying a gallop to Turkey to guzzle some tasty Turkish chiddlers.

> [*The other* GIANTS *rumble their approval*]

BFG: That's the Bonecruncher. He is thinking Turkish chiddlers is juiciest chiddlers. They is tasting of . . .

SOPHIE: Turkey?

BFG: No! Turkish delight!

SOPHIE: Of course.

> [*The* BONECRUNCHER *bumps into the* FLESHLUMPEATER, *who roars threateningly, making the* BONECRUNCHER *cower*]

Who's that big, fierce one?

BFG: That's the Fleshlumpeater.

FLESHLUMPEATER: I is fancying getting my chompers round a handful of chiddlers from Wellington!

SOPHIE: Where's Wellington?

BFG: Your head is full of squashed flies. Wellington is in New Zealand.

SOPHIE: What do children in Wellington taste of?

BFG: Boots, of course.

SOPHIE: But boots taste horrid.

BFG: Rubbsquash! Boots taste bootiful!

SOPHIE: Ha ha.

BLOODBOTTLER: I could be murdering some chiddlers from England!
[*The other* GIANTS *roar their approval*]

SOPHIE: England?

BFG: That's the Bloodbottler. He is thinking the English chiddlers is tasting ever so wonderfully of crodscollop.

SOPHIE: I'm not sure I know what that means.

BFG: Meanings is not important. I cannot be

right all the time. Quite often I is left instead of right.

[*A row breaks out among the* GIANTS. *They grunt and push, arguing about where to go*]

Let's go back. You will be coming to an ucky-mucky end if any of them should ever be getting his gogglers upon you. You would be swallowed up like a piece of frumpkin pie, all in one dollop.

[*They return inside the cave*]

There. You is safe in here.

[*They freeze during the following action*]

CHILDCHEWER: 'Tis the witchy hour!

[*The others grunt their agreement and all begin a kind of war-dance. Suddenly they all stop*]

MEATDRIPPER: 'Tis time for supper!

[*All excitedly agree and lumber round again. They suddenly stop*]

GIZZARDGULPER: Human beans . . .

BONECRUNCHER: Turkish chiddlers . . .

FLESHLUMPEATER: Wellington chiddlers . . .

BLOODBOTTLER: English chiddlers . . .

ALL: Here we come!

[*Roaring excitedly, the* GIANTS *run towards*

the audience, pounding along on the spot. Eventually, after at least twenty paces, they stop and menacingly look about them, hungrily sniffing. Suddenly, with a whoop, they find some dolls, swoop on them, pick them up, throw them to each other, roaring in hungry anticipation. Suddenly they all hold the dolls aloft]

Human beans! Human chiddlers!
   [*They savagely mime eating the dolls, as though stuffing their mouths, tearing off limbs, chewing and chomping. Having gorged themselves, they happily sink to the floor and, as though in a drunken stupor, start snoring. Then their snores fade as the action returns to the cave*]

SOPHIE: I think eating children is horrible.

BFG: I has told you. I is not eating chiddlers. Not I! I is a freaky giant! I is a nice and jumbly giant! I is the BFG.

SOPHIE: The BFG?

BFG: The Big Friendly Giant! What is your name?

SOPHIE: My name is Sophie.

BFG: How is you doing, Sophie? [*He gently shakes hands with the* SOPHIE DOLL] Is you quite snuggly in your nightie, Sophie? You isn't fridgy cold?

SOPHIE: I'm fine.

BFG: I cannot help thinking about your poor mother and father. By now they must be jipping and skumping all over the house shouting, 'Hallo, hallo, where is Sophie gone?'

SOPHIE: I don't have a mother and father. They died when I was a baby.

BFG: You is a norphan?

SOPHIE: Yes.
[*The* BFG *carefully takes the* SOPHIE DOLL *from* SOPHIE *and holds it up to his eye level*]

BFG: Oh you poor little scrumplet. You is making me sad.

SOPHIE: Don't be sad. No one at the orphanage will be worrying much about me.

BFG: Was you happy there?

SOPHIE: I hated it. Mrs Clonkers locked me in the cellar once.

BFG: Why?

SOPHIE: For not folding up my clothes.

BFG: The rotten old rotrasper!

SOPHIE: It was horrid. There were rats down there.

BFG: The filthy old fizzwiggler! You is making me sadder than ever. [*He sobs, hands the* SOPHIE DOLL *back to* SOPHIE, *and sits on the stool*]

SOPHIE: Don't cry, BFG. Please.
    [*The* BFG *recovers a little*]

Listen, BFG, we can't just sit here and do nothing.

BFG: What is you meaning?

SOPHIE: We can't let any more children be eaten. We've got to stop those brutes.

BFG: Us? Redunculus and umpossible.

SOPHIE: [*Building to a climax*] Nonsense! It's up to us! We've got to save the children of the world.

    [*Curtain down*]

SNOZZCUMBER AND
FROBSCOTTLE

In the book, the BFG and Sophie are visited by only one giant – the Bloodbottler, but I thought that theatrically it would be interesting to have him accompanied by the Fleshlumpeater. Two can menace the BFG more effectively than one!

CHARACTERS
Narrator.

The BFG: wearing his shirt, waistcoat, trousers, belt and sandals.

Sophie: the actress and the Sophie doll both in night-dresses and glasses.

Bloodbottler *and* Fleshlumpeater: wearing half-masks or head-dresses, and suitable costumes – a sacking tunic, perhaps, or simple jeans and dark T-shirt.

SETTING
The BFG's cave: containing a table and stool; a cave entrance and shelving with dream jars would be effective, but are not essential.

SPECIAL PROPS

The snozzcumber: a large, marrow-like prop, as
    described in the book, knobbly with black and
    white stripes. It needs to divide in two, perhaps
    held together with 'Velcro'. It should look
    large enough for the Sophie doll to apparently
    'crawl' inside, by being manipulated *behind* it.

The frobscottle bottle: a large, opaque green
    bottle is probably best, with a cork stopper.

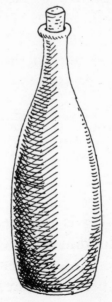

The downgoing bubbles can be imagined, unless an ingenious device can be made using torch-bulbs lighting up in sequence inside.

SOUND EFFECTS
These could be recorded or performed 'live' from offstage.

During the slow-motion sequence an eerie drone from an electronic keyboard could be effective.

When the Sophie doll flies through the air, an ascending, then descending, whistle would help the moment.

A fizzing noise when the cork is removed from the frobscottle bottle.

Whizzpoppers: loud, rude 'raspberry' noises with a popping sound on the end. The BFG's whizzpoppers should be full and vulgar. Sophie's could be more pinched and genteel!

Music for tension could be useful during the sinister moments.

LIGHTING
No special lighting is required, but if possible the lights should dim somewhat when Blood-bottler and Fleshlumpeater enter the cave, and fade up again when they leave. A special effect,

such as a revolving sequence of lights, could be effective during the slow-motion section.

The pop of each whizzpopper could be accompanied by a bright flash.

SNOZZCUMBER AND FROBSCOTTLE

First a NARRATOR *should set the scene.* (NB *If required,* SOPHIE *could speak the narration, showing the* SOPHIE DOLL, *and then 'enter' the scene*)

NARRATOR: Sophie has been snatched from the dormitory window of her orphanage by the Big Friendly Giant, who carries her off to Giant Country. Sophie discovers that all the other giants who live there enjoy eating human beings. Luckily she has been snatched by the only giant who does not . . .

> [*Curtain up. The* BFG *is standing by his table, looking down at the* SOPHIE DOLL, *who stands on the table, manipulated by* SOPHIE, *who kneels on the floor, and speaks her lines 'through' the doll*]

SOPHIE: BFG, tell me – if you don't eat humans, what *do* you eat?

BFG: [*Sitting*] That, little Sophie, is a squelching tricky problem. In this sloshflunking Giant Country, happy eats like pineapples and pigwinkles is simply not growing. Nothing is growing except for one extremely icky-poo vegetable. It is called the snozzcumber.

sophie: The snozzcumber? There's no such thing.

bfg: Is you calling me a fibster?

sophie: Well . . .

bfg: [*Getting cross*] Just because you has not *seen* something isn't meaning it isn't existing. What about the great squizzly scotch-hopper?

sophie: I beg your pardon?

bfg: And the humplecrimp?

sophie: What's that?

bfg: And the wraprascal? And the crumpscoddle?

sophie: Are they animals?

bfg: They is *common* animals. Swipe my swoggles! I is not a very know-all giant myself, but it seems to me you is an absolutely know-nothing human bean. Your brain is full of rotten-wool.

sophie: You mean cotton-wool.

bfg: [*Grandly*] What I mean and what I say is two different things. [*He stands*] I will now show you the repulsant snozzcumber.

[*The* bfg *finds a huge black and white striped,*

knobbly, cucumber-shaped vegetable, rather like
a giant's club]

SOPHIE: Gosh. It doesn't look very tasty.

BFG: It's disgusterous! It's sickable! It's maggot-
wise! [*He breaks it in two*] Try some.
[*He holds one half towards the* SOPHIE
DOLL]

SOPHIE: Pooh! No, thank you.

BFG: There's nothing else to guzzle. Have a go.
[*The* SOPHIE DOLL *nibbles some*]

SOPHIE: Uggggggggh! Oh no! It tastes of
frogskins. And rotten fish.

BFG: [*Roaring with laughter*] Worse than that! To
me it is tasting of clockcoaches and slime-
wanglers.

SOPHIE: Do I really have to eat it?

BFG: Unless you is wanting to become so thin
you will be disappearing into a thick ear.

SOPHIE: Into *thin air*. A thick ear is something
quite different.

BFG: [*Going to answer back, but checking himself*]
Words is oh such a twitch-tickling problem to
me. I know exactly what words I is wanting

to say, but somehow they come out all squiff-squiddly.

SOPHIE: That happens to everyone.

BFG: [*Sadly*] Not like it happens to me. I is speaking the most terrible wigglish.

SOPHIE: I think you speak beautifully.

BFG: [*Brightening*] You do? You is not twiddling my leg?

SOPHIE: No. I love the way you talk.

BFG: How wondercrump. How whoopsey-splunkers. Thank you, Sophie.
    [*Sudden thumping and shouting interrupts them*]

BLOODBOTTLER: [*Off*] Runt! Runt?

FLESHLUMPEATER: [*Off*] What is you up to, runt?

BFG: Quick, Sophie, hide.

SOPHIE: [*Narrating, as she hides the* SOPHIE DOLL *behind the snozzcumber on the table*] Sophie hid behind the snozzcumber.
    [BLOODBOTTLER *and* FLESHLUMPEATER *enter*]

BLOODBOTTLER: Aha!

FLESHLUMPEATER: Aha!

[*They stand threateningly above the* BFG, *who sits at the table trying to look calm*]

BFG: Hallo, Bloodbottler. Good day, Fleshlumpeater.

BLOODBOTTLER: Don't hallo good day us, runt.

FLESHLUMPEATER: We is hearing you jabbeling.

BLOODBOTTLER and FLESHLUMPEATER: [*Together*] Who is you jabbeling to, runt?

BFG: I is jabbeling to myself.

BLOODBOTTLER: Pifflefizz!

FLESHLUMPEATER and BLOODBOTTLER: [*Together*] You is talking to a human bean!

BFG: No, no!

BLOODBOTTLER: Yus!

FLESHLUMPEATER: Yus!

BLOODBOTTLER: We is guessing you has snitched away a human bean and brought it back to your bunghole as a pet!

FLESHLUMPEATER: So now we is winkling it

out and guzzling it as extra snacks before
supper!

[*They start sniffing and searching. The* BFG
tries to conceal the SOPHIE DOLL]

BFG: [*Nervously*] There's no one here. Why don't
you leave me alone?

BLOODBOTTLER: [*Threateningly*] Piffling little
swishfiggler!

FLESHLUMPEATER: Squimpy little pogswizzler!

BLOODBOTTLER and FLESHLUMPEATER: [*Together, sniffing and searching*] Where is it? Where
is it?

[*They freeze*]

SOPHIE: [*Narrating, and manipulating the* SOPHIE
DOLL, *making it look as though she goes inside the
snozzcumber, but in fact taking it* behind] Terrified, Sophie scooped out some slimy snozzcumber seeds and, unseen by the BFG, crawled
inside the pongy vegetable.

[BLOODBOTTLER *and* FLESHLUMPEATER
see the snozzcumber and move towards it. The
BFG *goes to protect the* SOPHIE DOLL, *but is
surprised when he cannot see her*]

BLOODBOTTLER: So this is the filthing rotsome
glubbage you is eating!

FLESHLUMPEATER: You must be cockles to be guzzling such rubbsquash!

BFG: Snozzcumbers is scrumdiddlyumptious.

BLOODBOTTLER: Human beans is juicier.

BFG: Try some. It's glumptious.

FLESHLUMPEATER: You is not switchfiddling us, is you?

BFG: Never. Vegitibbles is very good for you.

BLOODBOTTLER: Mmm. Just this once we is going to taste these rotsome eats of yours.

FLESHLUMPEATER: But if it is filthsome, we is smashing it over your sludgy little head!
    [*They each pick up half the snozzcumber.* SOPHIE *hides the* SOPHIE DOLL *behind* BLOODBOTTLER. *The action goes into slow motion*]

SOPHIE: [*Narrating*] Sophie felt herself being lifted up and up and up. She clung on desperately to stop herself falling out.
    [BLOODBOTTLER *and* FLESHLUMPEATER *mime taking a bite*]

Suddenly there was a crunch as the Bloodbottler bit a huge hunk off the end. Sophie saw his yellow teeth clamping together, then, utter darkness. She was in his mouth. Terrified, she waited for the next crunch . . .

> [*In slow motion,* BLOODBOTTLER *and* FLESHLUMPEATER *splutter with the horrible taste*]

BLOODBOTTLER: Eeeeeowtch!

FLESHLUMPEATER: Ughbwelch!
> [*They spit*]

SOPHIE: [*Narrating*] All the great lumps of snozzcumber, as well as Sophie herself, went shooting out across the cave.

> [*She manipulates the* SOPHIE DOLL, *slowly wheeling it in an arc from* BLOODBOTTLER'S *mouth to the floor. Then she lies down with it.* BLOODBOTTLER *and* FLESHLUMPEATER *snap out of slow motion*]

BLOODBOTTLER: You little swinebuggler!

FLESHLUMPEATER: You little pigswiller!

BLOODBOTTLER and FLESHLUMPEATER: [*Together*] It's disgusterous!

> [*They hit the* BFG *on the head with the snozzcumber halves*]

BFG: [*Rubbing his head*] You is not loving it?

BLOODBOTTLER: You must be buggles to be swalloping slutch like that!

FLESHLUMPEATER: Every night you could be galloping off happy as a hamburger and gobbling juicy human beans.

BFG: Eating human beans is wrong and evil! You is revoltant!

BLOODBOTTLER: And you is an insult to the giant peoples! You is not fit to be a giant!

FLESHLUMPEATER: You is a pibbling little pitsqueak! You is a . . . a . . . a cream puffnut!
[BLOODBOTTLER *and* FLESHLUMPEATER *exit, bellowing*]
[*The* BFG *checks they have gone*]

BFG: [*Whispering*] Sophie? Where is you, Sophie?

SOPHIE: I'm here.
[*The* BFG *finds the* SOPHIE DOLL *on the floor and tenderly picks her up*]

BFG: Oh, I is so happy to be finding you all in one lump.

SOPHIE: I was in the Bloodbottler's mouth!

BFG: What?

SOPHIE: I hid in the snozzcumber.

BFG: And I was telling him to eat it! You poor little chiddler, forgive me. Oho! You is needing some frobscottle to make you better.

[*He brings the* SOPHIE DOLL *to the table (followed by* SOPHIE)]

SOPHIE: Frobscottle?

BFG: Frobscottle. [*He proudly finds a bottle of green liquid*] I drink it lots. Delumptious, fizzy frobscottle!

[*He removes the stopper. There is a fizzing sound. If possible, bubbles are seen going downwards*]

SOPHIE: Hey, look! It's fizzing the wrong way!

BFG: What is you meaning?

SOPHIE: Downwards. In our fizzy drinks, like Coke and Pepsi, the bubbles go upwards.

BFG: Flushbunking rubbsquash!

SOPHIE: They do!

BFG: Upwards is the wrong way.

SOPHIE: Why?

BFG: If you is not seeing why, you must be as quacky as a duckhound! Upgoing bubbles is a catasterous disastrophe.

SOPHIE: But why?

BFG: Listen. When you is drinking this cokey drink of yours, it is going straight down into your tummy. Is that right? Or is it left?

SOPHIE: It's right.

BFG: And the bubbles is going also into your tummy. Right or left?

SOPHIE: Right again.

BFG: If the bubbles is fizzing upwards, they will all come swishwiffling up your throat and out of your mouth and make a foulsome belchy burp!

SOPHIE: That's often true. But what's wrong with a little burp now and again? It's sort of fun.

BFG: Burping is filthsome. Us giants is never doing it.

SOPHIE: But with *your* drink . . .

BFG: Frobscottle.

SOPHIE: With frobscottle, the bubbles in your tummy will be going *downwards* and that could have a far nastier result.

BFG: Why nasty?

SOPHIE: Because they'll be coming out some-
where else with an even louder and ruder noise.

BFG: A whizzpopper! Us giants is making whizz-
poppers all the time! Whizzpopping is a sign
of happiness. It is music in our ears!

SOPHIE: But it's . . . it's rude!

BFG: But you is whizzpopping, is you not, now
and again?

SOPHIE: Everyone is . . . whizzpopping. Kings
and queens, film stars, even little babies. But
where I come from, it's not polite to talk
about it.

BFG: Redunculous! If everyone is making whizz-
poppers, then why not talk about it? Now,
let's be having a swiggle and seeing the result!
[*The* BFG *drinks from the bottle. Pauses. Then
ecstasy fills his face. A very loud whizzpopper
nearly shoots him in the air*]

Whoopee!
[*And another*]

Wheeee!
[*And another*]

Wheeeeeeee!
[SOPHIE *laughs, in spite of herself*]

Have some yourself.

SOPHIE: Well . . .

BFG: Go on. It's gloriumptious!
[*He holds the bottle to the* SOPHIE DOLL'*s mouth. Pause*]

SOPHIE: It's lovely.

BFG: Just wait!
[*Suddenly a whizzpopper propels the* SOPHIE DOLL *into the air. Then a succession of whizz-poppers sends her somersaulting up and over, over and up*]

SOPHIE: Wheee! Wheeeeee!
[*The* BFG *roars with laughter. Eventually both settle, the* SOPHIE DOLL *in the* BFG'*s arms*]

BFG: [*Yawning*] Time for a snoozy sleep. Good night, Sophie.

SOPHIE: [*Sleepily*] That was fun. Goodnight, BFG.
[SOPHIE *curls up at the* BFG'*s feet*]

[*Curtain down*]

DREAM-CATCHING AND DREAM-WATCHING

This is probably the most ambitious BFG play to perform, offering opportunities for a large cast. But it need not be difficult to stage.

CHARACTERS

Sophie: the actress manipulates a Sophie doll to represent Sophie; both would best be dressed in night-dress and glasses.

The BFG: wearing his cloak, shirt, waistcoat, belt, trousers and sandals.

The Giants: Fleshlumpeater, Bloodbottler, Bonecruncher, Childchewer, Meatdripper and Gizzardgulper (all with speaking roles).

Other Giants: if required. All giants should wear masks or head-dresses, and perhaps tunics.

Miss Plumridge: an elderly, humourless teacher, who could wear a cardigan and skirt.

Rebecca: a schoolgirl.

A Class of Children: as many as practicable, all dressed in uniform or everyday dress.

The Headmaster: stern, wearing a suit, and, if required, a gown and mortar-board.

Mummy: a voice from offstage.

Sam: a schoolboy.

Dad: a pompous man, dressed in a bath-towel.

SETTING
As for *Sophie in Giant Country*, the cave on one side (not taking up too much room). The remainder of the acting area can be empty.

SPECIAL PROPS
The Sophie doll or puppet.

The BFG's dream jars: these should be on shelves in his cave. If possible they should be

painted different colours to represent different dreams. It would be most effective if they contained lights to make them glow. (The three jars the BFG uses to catch his dreams in Dream Country should look empty at first, then coloured when filled with a dream. A battery-operated bulb inside could achieve this, or the jar could be painted on one side with colour, and on the other with silver, to appear opaque. By turning each jar round, the BFG can make it look full. Each jar should have a stopper.)

A suitcase to contain three jars.

YOU COULD PACK
SUITCASE WITH
POLYSTYRENE WITH
HOLES CUT OUT
IN SHAPES OF
JARS TO PREVENT
THEM RATTLING

A fishing-net: in which the BFG catches his dreams.

A bed: for the dream-watching sequences, a bed upstage could be useful, though it is not essential. All the action is best mimed, so a blackboard and telephone are not necessary; similarly Sam should mime doing his homework.

SOUND EFFECTS

Suitable atmospheric music could be played in the Dream Country scene, and in the dream-watching sequence, but it is by no means essential.

A whistling-wind effect could help suggest the journey to Dream Country, the return, and the journey to Buckingham Palace.

A telephone bell (live or on tape, or even vocalized by an actor offstage!).

Exciting music could enhance the 'dream-mixing'.

LIGHTING

No special lighting is necessary, but it would be effective to be able to cross-fade between the cave and the other acting area. And Dream Country would benefit from coloured, moving lights and by the 'swirling mist' effect of dry ice. But, again, these are not essential.

DREAM-CATCHING AND
DREAM-WATCHING

Curtain up.

The BFG's *cave is on one side. On the other side, as though in the open air, the* GIANTS *are sprawled asleep. Before the play proper begins, the actress playing* SOPHIE *sets the scene. She carries the* SOPHIE DOLL.

SOPHIE: [*Narrating; introducing the* SOPHIE DOLL] This is Sophie. She has been snatched from her orphanage by a giant. Luckily he is the Big Friendly Giant, who cares for Sophie and prevents her from being eaten by the unfriendly giants who also live in Giant Country. Early one morning, in the BFG's cave, Sophie is still asleep. But the BFG is busy . . .

> [SOPHIE *goes to the cave, puts the* SOPHIE DOLL *on the table in a sleeping position, then lies on the floor. The* BFG *enters wearing his cloak. He takes three 'empty' jars from the shelves and places them in his suitcase, then he goes to leave.* SOPHIE *wakes up and, kneeling by the table, lifts the* SOPHIE DOLL *as though she is waking up too*]

SOPHIE: BFG?

BFG: [*Stopping*] Yes.

SOPHIE: Where are you going?

BFG: I is going to work.

SOPHIE: Back where I live? Blowing your trumpet thing?

BFG: [*Shocked*] You is seeing me blowing?

SOPHIE: Yes. What were you doing?

BFG: Is I trusting you?

SOPHIE: Of course.

BFG: Well, then. I, Sophie, is a dream-blowing giant. I blows dreams into the bedrooms of sleeping chiddlers. Nice dreams. Lovely golden dreams. Dreams that is giving the dreamers a happy time.

SOPHIE: Gosh.

BFG: See these jars? I is keeping the dreams in them.
   [*He carries the* SOPHIE DOLL *to look*]

SOPHIE: These are all dreams? But where do you get them?

BFG: I collect them.

SOPHIE: Collect them? That's impossible.

BFG: You isn't believing in dreams?

SOPHIE: Well, of course, but . . .

BFG: Listen. Dreams is very mysterious things. They is floating around in the air, like wispy-misty bubbles, searching for sleeping people. Come on. I is showing you. You is coming dream-collecting with me!

SOPHIE: [*Loudly*] Really? Yes, please!

BFG: Shhh! Hold your breaths and cross your figglers. Here we go!
[*He tucks the* SOPHIE DOLL *in his cloak, takes his suitcase and his fishing-net, and sets off from the cave.* SOPHIE *observes the following action from the side. The other* GIANTS *begin to snore as the* BFG *leaves the cave. The* BFG *creeps past them, treading carefully between their sprawled limbs. Just as we think he has negotiated them . . .*]

FLESHLUMPEATER: Ho-ho there, runt!

BLOODBOTTLER: Ho-ho there, little grob-squiffler!

BFG: [*Trying to be casual*] Ho-ho there. Has you had a good feasting?
[*The other* GIANTS *are waking*]

FLESHLUMPEATER: We has had a glumptious gorging!

BLOODBOTTLER: In Sweden!

BONECRUNCHER: We is liking the Sweden sour taste!
  [*The* GIANTS *laugh*]

FLESHLUMPEATER: Where is you going, runty one?
  [*He grabs the* BFG]

BLOODBOTTLER: Where is you splatch-winkling away to?
  [*He too grabs the* BFG]

BFG: [*Nervously*] Be so kind as to be letting go.
  [*The other* GIANTS *advance*]

BONECRUNCHER: Let's be having him!

FLESHLUMPEATER: To you, Bonecruncher!
  [*He pushes him towards* BONECRUNCHER. *The* GIANTS *roughly push him one to another, snatch his fishing-net and throw it back and forth too*]

BONECRUNCHER: To you, Meatdripper!

MEATDRIPPER: To you, Gizzardgulper!

GIZZARDGULPER: To you, Childchewer!

CHILDCHEWER: To you, Bonecruncher!

[*They laugh as the* BFG, *feverishly hanging on to his suitcase, grabbing back his fishing-net, and struggling to keep the* SOPHIE DOLL *concealed, is shoved to and fro*]

SOPHIE: [*Narrating*] Inside the BFG's cloak, Sophie clung on for dear life. At last the other giants tired of their game.

FLESHLUMPEATER: Run away, little runt!
[*Stunned, the* BFG *starts to stagger away*]

BLOODBOTTLER: Troggy little twit!

BONECRUNCHER: Shrivelly little shrimp!

MEATDRIPPER: Mucky little midget!

GIZZARDGULPER: Squaggy little squib!

CHILDCHEWER: Grobby little grub!
[*Laughing, the* GIANTS *exit. The* BFG *checks the* SOPHIE DOLL *is all right under his cloak, then exits*]

[*Optional:* SOPHIE, *as narrator, comes to the centre. We hear the sound of a whistling wind as swirls of mist envelop the stage. Coloured lights glow and dance on the smoke. This is to suggest Dream Country*]

SOPHIE: The BFG, clutching Sophie tight to his chest, ran and ran, leaped and galloped and flew . . . till at last . . .

[*The* BFG *enters. He takes the* SOPHIE DOLL *from his cloak.* SOPHIE *takes the doll and manipulates it once more*]

BFG: We is here!

SOPHIE: Where?

BFG: We is in Dream Country. Where all dreams is beginning.

[*Perhaps electronic sounds or music create a mysterious mood.* SOPHIE *and the* SOPHIE DOLL *look on as the* BFG *opens his suitcase, then watches, waits, and suddenly spies a floating dream. He slowly advances with his net, takes aim, then, with a swooping motion, leaps in the air and 'catches' the dream. Delighted, he transfers the dream to a jar, which lights up with a golden glow as he corks it. (See the special props section)*]

[*Another watchful wait, then a sighting. An energetic chase, at first 'missing' the dream, starting again, then triumphantly 'catching' it and transferring it to a jar, which glows pink*]

[SOPHIE *and the* SOPHIE DOLL *watch as the* BFG *waits once more. A third dream is sighted. Having caught it, the* BFG *has a struggle as it tries to escape the net. He tames it finally, and transfers it, using all his strength, to a jar, which glows green*]

[*Placing the jars in the suitcase and snapping it shut, the* BFG *takes the* SOPHIE DOLL, *puts her under his cloak, and exits. (Optional: The sound of a whistling wind returns.)* SOPHIE *returns to the* BFG'S *cave*]

SOPHIE: [*Narrating*] By the time the BFG and Sophie arrived back at the cave, darkness was beginning to fall.
[*The* BFG *enters the cave, puts his suitcase on the table, and carefully takes the* SOPHIE DOLL *from under his cloak.* SOPHIE *takes her and manipulates her once more, making her stand on the table, watching as the* BFG *removes his cloak, then opens the suitcase*]

BFG: Let us see what dreams we is catching! [*He holds up the golden jar*] Oh my! It's a phizz-wizard! A golden phizzwizard!

SOPHIE: Is that good?

BFG: The best. This will be giving some chiddler a very happy night when I is blowing it in.

SOPHIE: How can you tell?

BFG: I is hearing the dream's special music. I is understanding it.

SOPHIE: Gosh.

BFG: Shall I be showing Sophie this dream?

SOPHIE: Oh, yes please. But how?

BFG: Concentratiate. Watch and be listening!
> [*As they stare at the jar, the dream is acted out on the other side.* REBECCA *enters and lies down, asleep. She could be on a bed, but this is not essential. Her head starts to turn from side to side*]

REBECCA: I'm dreaming . . . I'm dreaming . . . I'm [*She opens her eyes, then stands and walks forwards. She acts out her dream*] at school . . . in class . . . and my teacher, Miss Plumridge, is droning on in a very boring way about William the Conqueror and the Battle of Hastings . . .
> [*Meanwhile,* MISS PLUMRIDGE *and the other* CHILDREN *in the class have entered. The* CHILDREN *sit, as though in class. (No need for chairs; on the floor is fine.)* MISS PLUMRIDGE *mimes talking to them and writing on the blackboard.* REBECCA *sits down with the others*]
. . . when suddenly I can't help myself humming a little tune. [*She hums*]

MISS PLUMRIDGE: Rebecca, cease that humming this instant!

> [*The* CLASS *try unsuccessfully to muffle their sniggers*]

REBECCA: But I can't help myself humming my little tune, and I hum it louder . . . [*She hums it louder*]

MISS PLUMRIDGE: Rebecca, how dare you! I said stop . . .

> [REBECCA '*fluences*' MISS PLUMRIDGE, *who suddenly freezes. The other* CHILDREN *have joined in the humming*]

REBECCA: Suddenly she freezes, then slowly but surely she starts to dance!

> [MISS PLUMRIDGE *slowly starts to dance, unsure of what is happening to her. This builds into a wild, uncontrolled rock'n'roll kind of shake, arms flailing, legs kicking. The* CLASS *hums and 'la las' louder, thoroughly enjoying the fun. Suddenly the* HEADMASTER *bursts in. The humming stops, but* MISS PLUMRIDGE *goes on dancing*]

REBECCA: The Headmaster!

HEADMASTER: What's going on in here? [*He sees* MISS PLUMRIDGE] Miss Plumridge! How dare you dance in class. Go fetch your coat and leave this school for ever! You are sacked! You are a disgrace!

[REBECCA *'fluences' the* HEADMASTER. *He freezes as* REBECCA *starts to hum again. The others join in. Suddenly the* HEADMASTER *starts to dance. Unable to resist, he too starts jigging around, and builds up into a wild explosion of movement. The* CLASS *enjoy it even more when he starts jiving with* MISS PLUMRIDGE. *Both still look shocked. The* CLASS *clap in rhythm and join in the dance, still humming and 'la la-ing'. Eventually* MISS PLUMRIDGE *and the* HEADMASTER *dance off, followed by the* CLASS. REBECCA *returns to her sleeping position*]

MUMMY: [*Off*] Rebecca!

REBECCA: Then suddenly I hear Mummy's voice . . .

MUMMY: [*Off*] Wake up! Your breakfast is ready!

[REBECCA *jolts upright and looks disappointed, then, remembering her dream, roars with laughter as she exits. Over in the cave, the* BFG *and* SOPHIE *gaze at the golden jar, and laugh too*]

SOPHIE: What a funny dream!

BFG: It's a ringbeller! A whoppsy!

[*He places the golden jar on the shelf*]

SOPHIE: Can we see another one? Please?

BFG: We can.

[*He takes the pink one from the suitcase. They stare at it*]

Oho! This is a pink dinghummer! Concentratiate! Watch and be listening!

[*Once again the dream is acted out on the other side.* SAM *enters and lies down, asleep. Suddenly his head starts to turn from side to side*]

SAM: I'm dreaming . . . I'm dreaming . . . I'm . . . [*He opens his eyes, then sits up, acting out his dream*] doing my homework, trying to work out a nasty bit of algebra, when suddenly . . .

[*A telephone rings and there is a voice from offstage –* DAD]

DAD: [*Off*] Sam! Answer that will you?

SAM: [*Calling*] I'm doing my homework, Dad.

DAD: [*Off*] I'm in the bath. Answer it!

SAM: [*Calling*] You said I had to do my homework, Dad.

[*A growl from* DAD, *who enters. His hair is wet and he is dressed in a bath-towel. He is very pompous*]

DAD: You'll pay for this, Sam. [*He picks up a real or mimed telephone receiver. The telephone stops ringing.*] Hallo. Simpkins here. [*Fiercely*] What . . . who? [*In amazement. When he hears the reply, he stands to attention and tries to smarten himself up*] Good evening, sir . . . yes, sir, how can I help you, sir? . . . Simpkins, sir . . . Ronald Simpkins . . . no, sir, Ronald, how can I help? . . . Who? . . . Well, yes, sir, there *is* a Sam Simpkins on this number, but surely it is me you wish to speak to, sir, not my little son? . . . Yes, sir, very well, sir, I will get him, sir. [*Turning to* SAM] Sam, it's for you.

SAM: Oh. Who is it, Dad?

DAD: The, er . . . the President of the United States.

SAM: [*Matter-of-factly*] Oh, right. [*He takes the receiver*]

DAD: [*Staggered*] Do you *know* the President of the United States?

SAM: [*With a smile*] No, but I expect he's heard of me.
     [*As he speaks on the telephone,* DAD *watches, eyes wide, mouth open in disbelief*]

[*Casually*] Hallo . . . Oh hi! . . . What's the problem? . . . OK, Mr President, leave it to me, I'll take care of it ... No, no, you'll bungle it all up if you do it your way ... A pleasure, Mr President. Now, I must get on with my algebra homework! Bye! Have a nice day!

[DAD *watches, bemused, as* SAM *puts down the telephone.* DAD *exits and* SAM *returns to lie down, asleep*]

DAD: [*Off*] Sam!

SAM: Then suddenly I hear Dad's voice.

DAD: [*Off*] Get up you lazy slob or you'll be late for school!

[SAM *jolts upright, and looks disappointed, then, remembering his dream, roars with laughter and exits. Over in the cave, the* BFG *and* SOPHIE *finish gazing at the pink jar and laugh*]

SOPHIE: That was good, too!

BFG: A dumhinger, I is telling you! [*He places the pink jar on the shelf and then takes the green one from his suitcase*] Now, what has we here? [*He looks at it. Suddenly ...*] Aaaaaah!

SOPHIE: What's the matter?

BFG: [*In alarm*] Oh no! I is catching ... a trogglehumper!

SOPHIE: A trogglehumper?

BFG: Yes. A bad, bad dream. A nightmare!

SOPHIE: Oh dear. What will you do with that?

BFG: I is never blowing it! If I do, then some poor little tottler will be having the most curdbloodling time! [*He puts it in his suitcase*] I is taking it back tomorrow. [*With a shudder*] Uggh! I is hating trogglehumpers.
> [*Suddenly a roar startles them, the offstage roar of the other* GIANTS]

Quick! Let's go look-see!
> [*As he and* SOPHIE *with the* SOPHIE DOLL *go to the cave entrance, the other* GIANTS *enter, full of energy and evil intent*]

BLOODBOTTLER: 'Tis the witchy hour. And I is starveling!

FLESHLUMPEATER: I is starveling rotten too!

GIANTS: And I! And I! And I! And I!

BONECRUNCHER: Let us go guzzle human beans!
> [*The* GIANTS *cheer their agreement*]

CHILDCHEWER: Let us flushbunk to England!

GIZZARDGULPER: England is a luctuous land and I is fancying a few nice little English chiddlers!

[*The* GIANTS *cheer*]

SOPHIE: Oh no!

BFG: Shhh!

MEATDRIPPER: I is knowing where there is a gigglehouse for girls and I is guzzling myself full as a frothblower!

FLESHLUMPEATER: And I knows a bogglebox for boys. All I has to do is reach in and grab myself a handful! English boys is tasting extra lickswishy!

[*The* GIANTS *cheer*]

BLOODBOTTLER: Be following me ... to England!

[*The* GIANTS *cheer and freeze on the spot. The* BFG *and* SOPHIE *with the* SOPHIE DOLL *return inside the cave*]

SOPHIE: It mustn't happen! We've got to stop them! We must chase after them and warn everyone in England they're coming!

BFG: Redunculus and *um*-possible. They is going twice as fast as me and they is finishing their guzzle before we is halfway. Besides, I is *never* showing myself to human beans. I is telling you, they will be putting me in the zoo with all the jiggyraffes and cattypiddlers.

SOPHIE: Nonsense.

BFG: And they will be sending *you* straight back to the norphanage. Grown-up human beans is not famous for their kindnesses. They is all squifflerotters and grinksludgers.

SOPHIE: That simply isn't true. Some of them are very kind indeed.

BFG: Who? Name one.

SOPHIE: The Queen of England. You can't call her a squifflerotter or a grinksludger.

BFG: Well . . .

SOPHIE: I've got it! Listen, BFG, we'll go to the Queen and tell her about the giants. She'll do something, I know she will.

BFG: She will never be believing in giants.

SOPHIE: [*With a sudden idea*] Then we'll make her *dream* about them. Can you make a person dream absolutely anything in the world?

BFG: Well, yes, I could be mixing any such dream, but . . .

SOPHIE: Then mix a dream fit for a Queen!
          [*The* BFG *thinks, then springs into action*]

BFG: Fit for a Queen!

[*He leaps to his shelves, taking down jars,
and pours small amounts from them into one
larger jar. He mixes the dream with a mechani-
cal whisk, then transfers it into a smaller jar.
He puts it in his suitcase, grabs his cloak and
the* SOPHIE DOLL. *He exits at speed.* SOPHIE
*watches the following action from the
side. The* GIANTS *break their freeze and
excitedly 'rev' themselves up in formation*]

GIANTS: England!

[*All exit, menacingly. The* BFG *enters, now
wearing his cloak, and starts running on the
spot, carrying his suitcase and the* SOPHIE
DOLL. *After a while he begins to slow down*]

SOPHIE: The BFG arrived in England. Sophie
directed him to London. To Buckingham
Palace!

[*The* BFG, *holding up the* SOPHIE DOLL,
*looks excitedly out front and starts walking
towards the audience as . . .*

the curtain falls]

SOPHIE AND THE QUEEN

This short play features three actresses and a narrator and needs a few simple props and costumes. The humour of the scene is helped if the Queen tries hard to keep her regal composure throughout all the emerging revelations, and if Mary becomes increasingly 'spooked'.

CHARACTERS

Narrator

Sophie: wearing her night-dress and glasses.

The Queen: even though she is in bed, she should probably be dressed in a dressing-gown. Her crown can be a simple one made of cardboard painted gold, or a more elaborate jewelled one. Her slippers are by the bed.

Mary: the Queen's maid; she wears a simple, smart maid's uniform with an apron.

SETTING

The Queen's bedroom can be done simply using a bed as the main feature. The window should be upstage; it could be an imagined window, using curtains which draw to suggest it. We do not need to see the door.

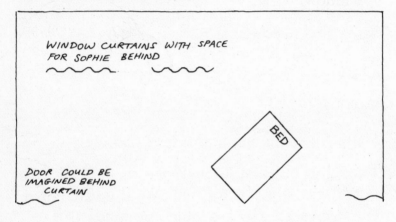

WINDOW CURTAINS WITH SPACE
FOR SOPHIE BEHIND

BED

DOOR COULD BE
IMAGINED BEHIND
CURTAIN

AUDIENCE

SPECIAL PROPS

The Queen's early-morning tea-tray: this would look best if it were silver, with a white cloth. On it should be a silver teapot and milk-jug, with a cup and saucer. These could be fastened loosely to the cloth or tray to stop them breaking when the tray is dropped.

A newspaper: *The Times*, probably!

A large BFG head: at the end of the scene, this
should appear at the window. It could be a
large cut-out on a pole, slowly pushed into
position between the curtains or behind the
window.

SOUND EFFECTS
The tick-tock of a clock could be recorded, or
played offstage on a xylophone. You might try
some dawn bird-song too.

For the door knock, if a real door is not used,
try banging a hammer on a piece of wood; or
tapping knuckles on the floor.

BFG footsteps and voice might best be recorded. Big, booming footsteps, followed by a big, booming voice. If performed live, try to make it sound as 'big' as possible.

LIGHTING

If lighting is available, the night-time lighting should allow the Queen's face to be visible for her bad dream.

Dawn should fade up slowly to a bright state.

A black-out at the end would be effective.

SOPHIE AND THE QUEEN

NARRATOR: Sophie and the Big Friendly Giant have overheard the other giants saying that they will flushbunk to England to guzzle lots of lickswishy chiddlers. Sophie decides they must tell the Queen of England, who will surely help. To make her believe in giants, the BFG has blown a special dream into the Queen's bedroom window at Buckingham Palace. And he has placed Sophie behind the curtains.

[*Curtain up. The* QUEEN *is in bed, her crown nearby. It is night-time. After a pause, the* QUEEN'*s head tosses from side to side as she dreams*]

QUEEN: [*Talking in her sleep*] Oh no! No! Don't! Someone stop them! Don't let them do it! It's horrible! Please stop them! It's ghastly! No! No! No!

[*As she drifts back to peaceful sleep, a tick-tock sound effect suggests the passing of time, and lighting suggests the coming of dawn. There is a sudden knock on the door.* MARY, *the* QUEEN'*s maid, enters carrying a tray with breakfast things and a newspaper*]

MARY: Good morning, Your Majesty. Your early-morning tea.

[*The* QUEEN *wakes up*]

QUEEN: Oh, Mary! I've just had the most frightful dream! It was awful!

MARY: Oh, I *am* sorry, ma'am. But don't be distressed. You're awake now.

QUEEN: I dreamt, Mary, that girls and boys were being snatched out of their beds at boarding-school and were being eaten by the most ghastly giants!

[MARY *pays attention*]

The giants were putting their arms in through the dormitory windows and plucking the children out with their fingers. It was all so . . . so *vivid*, Mary. So *real*.

[MARY *has been staring in amazement. The crockery on the tray rattles*]

Mary! What is it?

[*Suddenly* MARY *drops the tray with a clatter*]

Mary!

MARY: Sorry, Your Majesty . . .

QUEEN: I think you'd better sit down at once. You're as white as a sheet.

[MARY *sits on the edge of the bed*]

You mustn't take it so hard, Mary, just because I've had an awful dream.

MARY: That ... that isn't the reason, ma'am ... [*She reaches for the newspaper*] Look, ma'am! Look at the front page! The headlines!

QUEEN: [*Unfolding the newspaper*] Great Scott! [*She reads ...*] 'Children vanish mysteriously from boarding-school beds. Bones found underneath dormitory windows!' [*She gasps as she scans the small print*] Oh, how ghastly! It's absolutely frightful! Those *poor* children!

MARY: But, ma'am ... don't you see, ma'am ...

QUEEN: See what, Mary?

MARY: Those children were taken away almost exactly as you dreamt it, ma'am.

QUEEN: Not by giants, Mary.

MARY: No, ma'am. But the rest of it. You dreamt it and ... and ... and it's happened. For real! Oooh, it's spooky, ma'am. That's why I came over all queer.

QUEEN: I'm coming over a bit queer myself, Mary.

MARY: It gives me the shakes, ma'am, when

something like this happens, it really does. [*She tidies up the tray*]

QUEEN: I *did* dream about those children, Mary. It was clear as crystal.

MARY: I'm sure you did, ma'am.

QUEEN: [*Lightening the mood*] I don't know how *giants* got into it. That was rubbish.

MARY: Shall I draw the curtains, ma'am? Then we shall all feel better. It's a lovely day.

QUEEN: Please do.
   [MARY *draws the curtains.* SOPHIE *is revealed*]

MARY: Aaaaaaaah!
   [SOPHIE *looks frightened. The* QUEEN *looks frightened.* MARY *looks frightened, but recovers first*]

What in the name of heaven do you think you're doing in here?

SOPHIE: Please, I ... [*She looks beseechingly towards the* QUEEN]

QUEEN: I don't believe it. I simply don't believe it.

MARY: I'll take her out, ma'am, at once.

QUEEN: [*Sharply*] No, Mary, don't do that. Tell me, is there *really* a little girl in a nightie by the window, or am I still dreaming?

MARY: You're wide awake, ma'am, and there's a little girl in a nightie by the window, though heaven only knows how she got there.

QUEEN: [*Remembering*] But I *know* how she got there. I dreamt that as well. A giant put her there.

[MARY *reacts with a gasp*]

Little girl, am I right?

SOPHIE: Yes, Your Majesty.

MARY: Well, I'll be jiggered. It can't be true!

QUEEN: And your name is . . .

[SOPHIE *goes to speak*]

Don't say it! Mary, come here.

[MARY *goes to the* QUEEN]

Her name is . . . [*She whispers in* MARY'*s ear*]

MARY: Impossible, ma'am, how could you know that? [*To* SOPHIE] What's your name, girl?

SOPHIE: My name is Sophie.

MARY: Aaaaaaaah! [*She clutches her heart, looking, mouth open in amazement, from* SOPHIE *to the* QUEEN *and back again*]

QUEEN: Told you. Come here, Sophie.
[SOPHIE *approaches. Perhaps the* QUEEN *puts on her crown*]

Sit down, dear.
[SOPHIE *sits on the* QUEEN'*s bed*]

Are you real?

SOPHIE: Yes, Your Majesty.

QUEEN: And did a giant really bring you here?

SOPHIE: Oh, yes, Your Majesty. He's out there in the garden now.
[MARY *shudders*]

QUEEN: Is he indeed? In the garden?

SOPHIE: He's a *good* giant, Your Majesty. The Big Friendly Giant. You needn't be frightened of him.

QUEEN: I'm delighted to hear it.

SOPHIE: He is my best friend.

QUEEN: How nice.

SOPHIE: Shall I call him for you?

QUEEN: [*After a pause*] Very well.
[SOPHIE *runs to the window*]

MARY: Is this wise, ma'am?

QUEEN: Slippers, Mary.
[MARY *fetches them, as the* QUEEN *gets out of bed. She puts them on*]

SOPHIE: [*Calling from the window*] BFG! Her Majesty the Queen would like to see you.
[*Pause.* MARY *and the* QUEEN *look at each other, not really expecting anything to happen*]

QUEEN: I don't see any giant.

SOPHIE: Please wait.

MARY: Shall I take the girl away now, ma'am?
[*Sudden heavy footsteps echo from outside the window.* MARY *and the* QUEEN *look in fearful anticipation. The footsteps stop. A voice booms . . .*]

BFG: [*Off*] Your Majester, I is your humbug servant.
[*Suddenly a huge* BFG *head appears at the window.* MARY *screams 'silently' and faints, unseen by the* QUEEN]

QUEEN: [*Taking things in her stride*] We are very pleased to meet you. Mary, ask Mr Tibbs to prepare breakfast for our two visitors. In the ballroom, I fancy. [*Pause*] Mary? [*She turns to see* MARY, *flat out on the floor*]

Oh.

[*Black-out or curtain down*]

BREAKFAST AT BUCKINGHAM PALACE

There are seven speaking roles and several interesting non-speaking roles in this play. The optional section before the dialogue starts offers an opportunity to introduce a team of palace staff, who busily scuttle round setting up the scene under the supervision of Mr Tibbs, the butler. They could bring in the table and lay it, set the chairs, and even bring on the BFG.

Although, in the book, Roald Dahl does not suggest that the Queens of England and Sweden are in full ceremonial dress, I think it helps the humour and the theatricality of the scene if they are! The Heads of the Army and Air Force should work together like toy soldiers, synchronizing their movements and being ultra pompous.

CHARACTERS

The BFG: because, in this play, the other characters are human-scale, the BFG has to be enormous! Ideally he would be a huge puppet seated, as in the book, on a chest of drawers on a piano, using a table-tennis table balanced on grandfather clocks as his table.

An easier way to suggest him is to imagine he is *offstage*, and everybody looking off and up when they talk to him!

A good compromise might be to paint a fairly tall flat with the BFG's 'table', and stand an

actor on top of a ladder behind it so that his head peeps over the top. Or a cut-out giant head could be held and manipulated above.

Narrator.

The Queen: ideally in full ceremonial dress.

Sophie: in her night-dress and glasses, but probably wearing an over-large dressing-gown (the Queen's?).

Mr Tibbs, the butler: in full morning-dress-style butler's rig.

Mary, the maid.

Undermaid.

More undermaids (optional).

Chef (optional).

Queen of Sweden: in full ceremonial dress.

Head of the Army
Head of the Air Force $\Big\}$ in uniform.

SETTING
The ballroom of Buckingham Palace could be very simply represented with an empty, curtained stage. A regal archway, through which

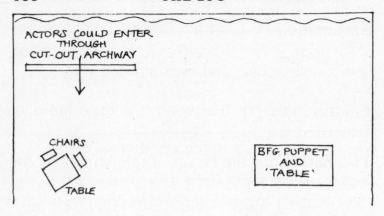

the characters could enter, would be effective, but is not essential.

A breakfast table with two chairs is on one side of the acting area.

The BFG, as described above, is on the other side.

SPECIAL PROPS

The breakfast table: with a bright, white table-cloth. Should have two place settings and maybe a toast-rack, with triangles of toast, and a butter-dish.

A giant-sized breakfast plate: probably made of papier mâché topped with 'joke' bacon, eggs and sausages.

A giant fork.

A small silver tray: with a portable telephone on it.

Another portable telephone: for the Queen of Sweden.

Two batons: for the Heads of the Army and Air Force to carry.

SOUND EFFECTS AND MUSIC

Regal music would be useful for the optional introduction to the scene.

A fanfare should herald the Queen's entrance.

A military drumroll should accompany the entrance of the Heads of the Army and Air Force.

The giant whizzpopper could be on tape, or performed live into a microphone! It should be loud and very rude!

The telephone bell could be on tape, or performed live with an electric bell. As the telephone is Swedish, use long single rings.

LIGHTING

No special lighting is required. However, if the optional introduction to the scene is used, with the palace staff preparing the ballroom for breakfast, it could be effective to do this in a 'blue wash' or in rather dim lighting, which would fade up when the Queen and Sophie enter.

A bright state is best for the main scene.

If possible, individual lights on the Queen and the Queen of Sweden would make the telephone conversation more effective.

The BFG's whizzpopper could be accompanied by flickering lights.

BREAKFAST AT BUCKINGHAM PALACE

NARRATOR: The Big Friendly Giant and Sophie have come to Buckingham Palace to ask the Queen to do something to stop the other giants making any more children-eating raids. Breakfast is served in the ballroom.

[*Curtain up. Regal music*]

[*The* BFG *is seated at his improvised table.* MR TIBBS *stands formally in attendance.* MARY, *the maid, and the* UNDERMAID (*or two other maids*) *finish laying the breakfast table for two people*]

[*A* CHEF *enters with a very large plate of bacon, eggs and sausages. He hands it politely to* MR TIBBS, *then exits.* MR TIBBS *tries to serve the plate to the* BFG, *but the table-top is too high*]

[*He has an idea and beckons on* MARY *and the* UNDERMAID, *who are carrying a step-ladder. They erect it alongside the* BFG, *and* MR TIBBS *climbs it, gives the* BFG *his breakfast, then comes down again.* MARY *and the* UNDER-MAID *remove the step-ladder*]

[*Fanfare. Enter the* QUEEN. *Ideally she should*

[*be in full rig – ballgown and crown. She might even have with her a corgi on a lead. She beckons on* SOPHIE, *who looks impressed as she enters the ballroom*]

[MR TIBBS *goes to seat the* QUEEN, *but she indicates that* SOPHIE *should be seated first.* MR TIBBS *helps* SOPHIE, *then the* QUEEN, *and then takes the corgi and hands it to the* UNDERMAID, *who leads it offstage*]

[*The* QUEEN, SOPHIE *and the* BFG *start their breakfast.* MR TIBBS *and* MARY (*holding a small tray with a portable telephone on it*) *stand formally in the background. The* UNDERMAID *can join them*]

[*The music finishes*]

[*NB If required, the action of the play could start here*]

BFG: By goggles, Your Majester, this stuff is making snozzcumbers taste like swatchwallop.

QUEEN: I beg your pardon?

SOPHIE: He has never eaten anything except snozzcumbers before, Your Majesty. They taste revolting.

QUEEN: They don't seem to have stunted his growth!

BFG: Where is the frobscottle, Majester?

QUEEN: The *what?*

BFG: Delumptious fizzy frobscottle! Everyone must be drinking it. Then we can all be whizzpopping happily together!

QUEEN: What *does* he mean? What is whizzpopping?

SOPHIE: Excuse me, Your Majesty. [*She goes to the* BFG] BFG, there is no frobscottle here and whizzpopping is strictly forbidden.

BFG: What? No whizzpopping? No glumptious music?

SOPHIE: Absolutely not.

QUEEN: If he wants to make music, please don't stop him.

SOPHIE: It's not exactly music . . .

BFG: Listen, I can whizzpop perfectly well *without* frobscottle if I is trying hard enough.

SOPHIE: No! Don't! Please!

QUEEN: When I'm up in Scotland, they play

the bagpipes outside my window while I'm eating. [*To the* BFG] Do play something.

BFG: I has Her Majester's permission!

[*After a moment's concentration, a very loud and long whizzpopper rents the air, perhaps causing the lighting to flicker. Everyone reacts*]

Whoopee! How's that, Majester?

QUEEN: I think I prefer the bagpipes.

[*But she smiles, to* SOPHIE'*s relief*]

Now, to business. Sophie, you have told me of your visit to Giant Country and of the giants' ghastly night-time children-eating raids. But before we decide what is to be done, I must confirm the facts. Big Friendly Giant, last night your . . . er . . . colleagues raided England. Where did they go the night before?

BFG: I think, Majester, they was galloping off to Sweden. They is liking the Sweden sour taste.

QUEEN: Right. Mr Tibbs, the telephone.

[MR TIBBS *approaches with a portable telephone on a silver tray*]

Thank you. [*She presses the dialling buttons and waits*]

[*A telephone rings. The lighting changes, staying on the* QUEEN *and coming up on an area the other*] *side of the stage. The* QUEEN OF SWEDEN *enters in full ceremonial dress. She holds a telephone*]

QUEEN OF SWEDEN: [*On the phone*] Hallo, Queen of Sweden here.

QUEEN: Good morning, it's the Queen of England. Is everything all right in Sweden?

QUEEN OF SWEDEN: Everything is terrible! Two nights ago, twenty-six of my loyal subjects disappeared. My whole country is in a panic!

QUEEN: They were eaten by giants. Apparently they like the sweet and sour taste of Swedes. So says the BFG.

QUEEN OF SWEDEN: I don't know *what* you're talking about. It's hardly a joking matter when one's loyal subjects are being eaten like popcorn.

QUEEN: They've eaten mine as well.

QUEEN OF SWEDEN: Who's *they*, for Heaven's sake?

QUEEN: Giants.

QUEEN OF SWEDEN: Look here, are you feeling all right?

QUEEN: It's been a rough morning. First I had a horrid nightmare, then the maid dropped my early-morning tea, and now I've a giant on the piano.

QUEEN OF SWEDEN: You need a doctor, quick!

QUEEN: I'll be all right. I must go now. Thanks for your help.

> [*The lights fade on the* QUEEN OF SWEDEN, *who exits. The* QUEEN *hands the telephone back to* MR TIBBS]

That proves it. Mr Tibbs, summon the Head of the Army and the Head of the Air Force immediately!

> [MR TIBBS *bows, clicks his fingers, and points to the entrance. Military drumroll as, immediately, the* HEADS OF THE ARMY *and* AIR FORCE, *in full military uniform, enter, carrying batons. They march in step, not seeing the* BFG. *They arrive at the* QUEEN's *table, stand to attention and salute*]

QUEEN: Good morning, gentlemen.

HEAD OF THE ARMY: What ho, Your Majesty!

HEAD OF THE AIR FORCE: Toodle pip, Your Majesty!

QUEEN: We have a job for you.

HEAD OF THE ARMY: Jolly good show, Your Majesty!

HEAD OF THE AIR FORCE: Whizzo prang, Your Majesty!

QUEEN: Now, you've read about the disappearing children?

HEAD OF THE ARMY: Jolly bad show, Your Majesty.

HEAD OF THE AIR FORCE: Bally disgrace, Your Majesty.

QUEEN: They were eaten.

HEAD OF THE ARMY and HEAD OF THE AIR FORCE: [*Together, scandalized*] Eaten?

QUEEN: By giants.
　　[*Pause*]

HEAD OF THE ARMY: Hold fire, Your Majesty.

HEAD OF THE AIR FORCE: Giants?

HEAD OF THE ARMY: No such fellas, Your Majesty.

HEAD OF THE AIR FORCE: Except in fairy-tales.

HEAD OF THE ARMY: Except in fairy-tales.

HEAD OF THE ARMY and HEAD OF THE AIR FORCE: [*Together*] Ha, ha, ha, ha, ha!

HEAD OF THE ARMY: Jolly good joke, Your Majesty.

HEAD OF THE AIR FORCE: Not April the first, is it?

HEAD OF THE ARMY and HEAD OF THE AIR FORCE: [*Together*] Ha, ha, ha, ha, ha!

QUEEN: Gentlemen, allow me to present the Big Friendly Giant. [*She indicates behind them*]

HEAD OF THE ARMY and HEAD OF THE AIR FORCE: [*Together*] Big Friendly Giant! Ha ha ha ha ha!
　　[*They turn. They see the* BFG]

　[*Together*] Aaaaaaaah!
　　[*They cling to each other in terror*]

BFG: How is you doing, gentlebunglers?

HEAD OF THE ARMY and HEAD OF THE AIR FORCE: [*Together*] A giant!

QUEEN: Indeed. Luckily a friendly one. His colleagues are not. Tonight those bloodthirsty brutes will be galloping off to gobble up another couple of dozen unfortunate wretches. They have to be stopped. Fast.

HEAD OF THE ARMY: Message received, Your Majesty!

HEAD OF THE AIR FORCE: Message understood, Your Majesty!

QUEEN: They must be brought back. Alive.

HEAD OF THE ARMY and HEAD OF THE AIR FORCE: [*Together*] Alive?

HEAD OF THE ARMY: But how, Your Majesty? I mean, giants . . .

HEAD OF THE AIR FORCE: They'd knock us down like ninepins!

HEAD OF THE ARMY: Absolutely.

HEAD OF THE AIR FORCE: Absolutely.

HEAD OF THE ARMY: Indisputably.

HEAD OF THE AIR FORCE: Indisputably.

BFG: Wait! Keep your skirts on! I has the answer.
　　[*The* HEADS OF THE ARMY *and* AIR FORCE *begin to react crossly*]

QUEEN: Let him speak.

BFG: Every afternoon all these giants is lying on the ground snoozling in the Land of Noddy.

HEAD OF THE ARMY: Land of Noddy? What's he prattling about?

SOPHIE: Land of Nod. Asleep. It's pretty obvious.

BFG: All you has to do is creep up on them and tie them up.

HEAD OF THE AIR FORCE: But how do we get the brutes back here?

BFG: You is having bellypoppers, is you not?

HEAD OF THE AIR FORCE: Are you being rude?

SOPHIE: He means helicopters.

HEAD OF THE AIR FORCE: Then why doesn't he say so? Of course we have bellypoppers . . . er, helicopters.

QUEEN: Then, gentlemen, get cracking.

HEAD OF THE ARMY: Yes, Your Majesty. Forward!

HEAD OF THE AIR FORCE: Chocks away! Roger and out!

[*The* HEADS OF THE ARMY *and* AIR FORCE *turn inward and bump into each other*]

[*Black-out or curtain down*]

THE GUNZLESWIPING OF THE GIANTS

Shadow puppets are particularly good at portraying 'big' scenes, which would be difficult to put on a stage. This play is very short, but effectively uses a large number of people as puppeteers, voices and sound-effects makers.

You will need a suitable screen at table or head height. A strong light source from behind silhouettes the puppets against the screen.

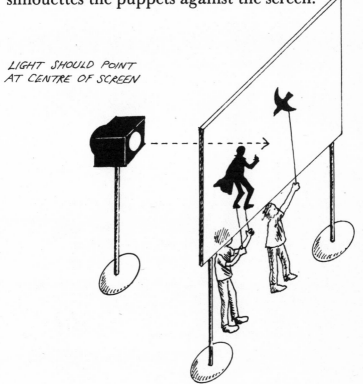

LIGHT SHOULD POINT
AT CENTRE OF SCREEN

Here is the play as the audience see and hear it. Afterwards we can look at the puppets in more detail, and ideas on performance.

THE GUNZLESWIPING OF THE GIANTS

NARRATOR: The Big Friendly Giant and Sophie have asked the Queen of England to stop the other giants' nightly children-eating raids. She orders the Head of the Army and the Head of the Air Force to set off for Giant Country and capture the giants while they sleep. The BFG and Sophie offer to lead the way.

[*Stirring Dam Busters-type music could help set the scene, as the screen lighting is turned on and the other lights are turned off. The music could continue 'under' the action*]

[*The distant roar of helicopter engines is heard. (This continues throughout the play at whatever volume is appropriate to suit the action)*]

[*A bird flies happily from left towards right. The bird sees something and squawks, flapping its wings in amazement*]

[*The* BFG, *running slow motion in big leaps, enters from right towards left. He carries a tiny* SOPHIE]

BFG: [*Echoing*] Follow, follow!

[*The bird flies upwards to avoid being hit by*

the BFG *as he runs across the screen and disappears*]

[*The helicopter engine noises grow louder. The bird flies lower again, then has another shock. It squawks, flaps its wings and flies upwards, narrowly avoiding the entrance of three helicopters, one by one, from right to left. The bird exits*]

[*The helicopters fly in formation, in a circular pattern. The helicopter engine noises fade to a background hum as voices are heard, as though through headphones*]

HEAD OF THE ARMY: Where the devil are we going?

HEAD OF THE AIR FORCE: I haven't the foggiest idea. We've flown clear off the map!

HEAD OF THE ARMY: Look! Look down!
[*The helicopters tip up at an angle, as though looking down. Loud snoring noises sound over the hum of the helicopter engines*]

Giants!

HEAD OF THE AIR FORCE: Stand by, chaps!
[*Three soldiers slowly descend from the helicopters on ropes, eventually dropping behind the limit of the screen. The snoring continues*]

[*A tick-tock noise suggests the passage of time. Perhaps the colour on the screen changes too*]

HEAD OF THE AIR FORCE: Winch away!
[*The ropes rise, pulling up two* GIANTS *each, trussed up horizontally, with the occasional moving limb. The soldiers are balanced on top. When all are visible, the voices of the* GIANTS *are heard, and continue as the helicopters move off and exit, carrying their giant cargo*]

FLESHLUMPEATER: I is flushbunkled!

CHILDCHEWER: I is splitzwiggled!

BONECRUNCHER: I is swogswalloped!

MEATDRIPPER: I is gunzleswiped!

GIZZARDGULPER: I is slopgroggled!

BLOODBOTTLER: I is crodsquinkled!
[*The helicopter engine noises fade, as the* BFG *enters from the right, bringing up the rear, carrying* SOPHIE]

BFG: Sophie, we has diddly diddly done it!

SOPHIE: Yes, BFG. We diddly diddly has!
[*They disappear and the lighting on the screen is turned off as the music rises, then fades*]

THE END

PUPPETS

The basic shapes can be made of cardboard cut from cardboard boxes. Here are some suggested designs and working methods:

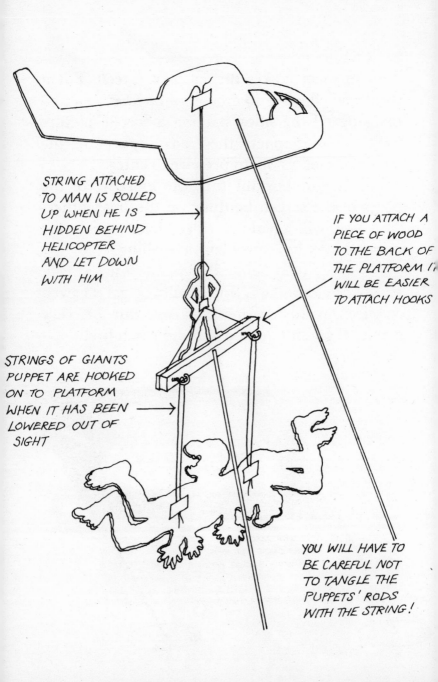

STRING ATTACHED TO MAN IS ROLLED UP WHEN HE IS HIDDEN BEHIND HELICOPTER AND LET DOWN WITH HIM

IF YOU ATTACH A PIECE OF WOOD TO THE BACK OF THE PLATFORM IT WILL BE EASIER TO ATTACH HOOKS

STRINGS OF GIANTS PUPPET ARE HOOKED ON TO PLATFORM WHEN IT HAS BEEN LOWERED OUT OF SIGHT

YOU WILL HAVE TO BE CAREFUL NOT TO TANGLE THE PUPPETS' RODS WITH THE STRING!

SCREEN

A linen sheet makes the simplest screen. But it would be effective to create a 'playing area', by blacking off the sides, making a sort of picture frame. The puppets then have space on the screen, out of vision, to prepare to enter.

NB It is important that the masking of the edges of the screen be done on the *front*; otherwise you will create a ridge, over which the puppets may have problems travelling.

If you wish to change the colour of the screen, try covering the light source with a 'gel' or even coloured tissue or crêpe paper. But be very careful it doesn't get too hot and catch fire!

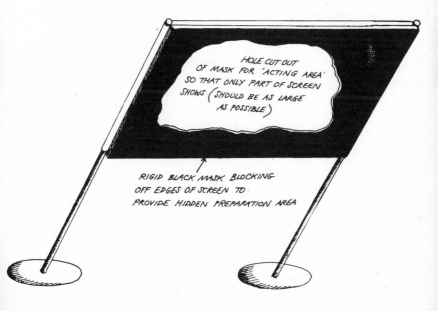

HOLE CUT OUT OF MASK FOR 'ACTING AREA' SO THAT ONLY PART OF SCREEN SHOWS (SHOULD BE AS LARGE AS POSSIBLE)

RIGID BLACK MASK BLOCKING OFF EDGES OF SCREEN TO PROVIDE HIDDEN PREPARATION AREA

VOICES

Apart from the scripted lines for the characters, everybody can join in the snoring.

The voices of the Head of the Army and the Head of the Air Force can appear distorted, as though through headphones, simply by holding noses!

A good bird squawk is required.

SOUND EFFECTS

The noise of wings fluttering could be made by paper or material rapidly made taut and then released by the hands.

A xylophone could make the tick-tock noise.

If it is not possible to have helicopter engine noises on tape, a group of you could vocalize them.

When Quentin Blake began to illustrate *The BFG*, he drew the giant wearing heavy boots. But neither Roald nor Quentin felt that boots looked quite right. A few days later, Quentin received a large package containing a battered old sandal – one of Roald's! – it was perfect for the BFG.

MORE ABOUT
The BFG

FOOTPRINTS

In the churchyard at Great Missenden, Buckinghamshire, big friendly giant footprints lead to Roald Dahl's grave.

THE BFG STAMP

To celebrate the BFG's 30th birthday in 2012, the Royal Mail issued a set of special-edition stamps – starring the BFG and Her Majesty the Queen!

**Take a tour of Roald Dahl's
scrumdiddlyumptious
official website with your
favourite characters at**

roalddahl.com

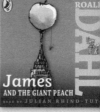

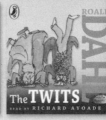

THERE'S MORE TO ROALD DAHL THAN GREAT STORIES . . .

Did you know that 10% of Roald Dahl's royalties* from this book go to help the work of the Roald Dahl charities?

Roald Dahl is famous for his stories and rhymes, but much less well known is how often he went out of his way to help seriously ill children. Today **Roald Dahl's Marvellous Children's Charity** helps children with the severest conditions and the greatest needs. The charity believes every child can have a more marvellous life, no matter how ill they are, or how short their life may be.

Can you do something marvellous to help others? Find out how at **www.roalddahlcharity.org**

You can find out about Roald Dahl's real-life experiences and how they found their way into his stories at the **Roald Dahl Museum and Story Centre** in Great Missenden, Buckinghamshire (the author's home village). The Museum is a charity that aims to inspire excitement about reading, writing and creativity. There are three fun and fact-packed galleries, with lots to make, do and see (including Roald Dahl's writing hut). Aimed at 6–12-year-olds, the Museum is open to the public and to school groups throughout the year.

Find out more at **www.roalddahlmuseum.org**

Roald Dahl's Marvellous Children's Charity (RDMCC) is a registered charity no. 1137409.
The Roald Dahl Museum and Story Centre (RDMSC) is a registered charity no. 1085853.
The Roald Dahl Charitable Trust is a registered charity no. 1119330 and supports the work of RDMCC and RDMSC.

* Donated royalties are net of commission